SELFIE DOODLE DOO!

SELFIE DOODLE DOO!

An introduction to my new friends

FRANK LANFRANCO

Illustrations by Frank Lanfranco

Selfie Doodle Publishing Waco, Texas and initial Distribution by Ingram Content and Publishing 2022

Copyright © 2022 by Frank Lanfranco Jr. Selfie Doo Publications Waco, Texas   PO Box 328 Hamilton Tx 76531   Initial Distribution by Ingram Content and Publishing.

All rights reserved. No part of this book may be reproduced in any manner whatsoever without written permission except in the case of brief quotations embodied in critical articles and reviews.

While we have made every effort to ensure the accuracy of the information in this book and its independence in content use we cannot be held liable for errors, omissions or inconsistencies.

First Printing, 2022

*Thank you to my friends and family
and the gift from God to accomplish this.
Thanks to Madison for the belief and push.*

Hi my name is Selfie Doodle Doo. And that's me
on the front cover. I am your funny chicken friend
who can appear in any digital photo or print you
can create with your mobile and home devices.
Invite me to go along with you, your family, and
friends as you explore and share the world with
all. I will put a smile on your face and others as
they enjoy your photos and backgrounds with my
simple click image in the
right hand corner.

What follows is the story of who I am and my
family history.

My story starts in England and with an
adventure voyage on the Mayflower. You have heard
the history of the Mayflower. Well my chicken
family was a part of that voyage. The Chicken
Doodle name had its start

with a farming family from a small village near Plymouth England. A farmer and his wife with the last name of Doodle. The Doodle's had a chick who they raised by hand and who became their pet. The Doodles had no children and the chick was very special to them. They called him Little Doodle Doo. Little Doodle Doo grew to be a great rooster and started his own family and kept the Doodle Doo name for all future Doodle Doo Chickens. All the chicks were given a first name followed by "Doodle Doo". I am a descendent of this great rooster and his family. That's the origin of my name , Selfie Doodle Doo.

One sunny morning, a traveler came calling at
the farm and wanted to purchase two Doodle Doo
chickens to take on a journey with him and others
to a new land. That land would become America in
time . The purpose of a chicken is obvious to this
day. They are proud to be of service to people and
provide meat and eggs for the nourishment and the
good health of all. These were to be the first Chicken
Doodle Doo's in the new land. They would grow the
Chicken Doodle Doo population and provide for the
future of the new land.

The journey would be on the ship Mayflower. The mission of the 42 pilgrims and the 60 others on board was to go to the new land to establish freedom and a new way of life as a country of people away from England and the single rule of the King of England.

The journey was 66 days and a hard one for most who had never been to sea. The first Doodle Doo

Chickens were going to America along side other farm animals on board with the travelers, They made the voyage and landed at Plymouth Rock in the new land.

Not having good shelters for the first winter, many of the travelers and animals lost their lives. We Chicken Doodle Doo's are a hardy stock and thankfully survived. Spring brought on a better climate and we were able to build a new camp and shelter.

This is where Mr. and Mrs. Chicken Doodle Doo met their first Native American friend. A friendly sort that was very curious about the chicken pair that roosted around the Pilgrim garden. Soon came the first two Doodle Doo chicks that would start the future growth of the Chicken Doodle Doo's in America. Of course as with all families, this family's birth was exciting to all.

The first fall brought on a celebration of the crops for the travelers and thanks for a new life in America. Mr. and Mrs. Chicken Doodle Doo and their chicks gave thanks too for being a part of the *future of what would become America. As you can see in the picture, that's a turkey in the pilgrims hands. Wild turkey was abundant in the New Land. And it became a tradition to serve.*

The tradition of this feast would become known as Thanksgiving Day. A great family holiday for all in America.

With the population of the New Land growing and as more immigrants came, the Doodle Doo Chicken families grew and started to spread to other parts and colonies. They became great providers for the new colonies .

*As time passed, there came a call by the
immigrants to fight for their freedom from the King
of England
Under the command of our future first president
General George Washington, they fought and
freedom was won for the New Land from England
and English King Rule.*

The Chicken Doodle Doo's are proud for making a great contribution in providing a source of food for the thousands of families in the battle for America's Freedom.
On July 4th 1776, the declaration of independence

from England was created and signed. This would lead to the Constitution that governs us through this day. Doodle Doo Chickens keep moving forward. Every year we celebrate our independence on the fourth of July.

Yankee Doodle Andy

When you hear a rooster call out with a loud
"Cock a Doodle Doo ", you will remember this story
and my family. That's my story. I hope you liked it.
.........Did you?

Hope to see you on the internet. Now that you know a little of my family history, it's time to ask your family about yours . Join me soon for new adventures in travel and making new friends around the world!!.

The End

You are welcome to use my image in your photos or prints. But please do not dishonor the name of the Doodle Doo's ! You will find me and my other selfie

character friends on facebook under
selfiedoodledoo.com

Images and story of Selfie Doodle Doo are for personal use only and not to be copied or used for commercial purposes under restriction of trade laws and copyright law. Photos used could be under copyright protection. Do not reproduce.

In Memory of Ma and Pa Doodle and Little Doodle

www.ingramcontent.com/pod-product-compliance
Lightning Source LLC
Chambersburg PA
CBHW040159110726

48005CB00018B/2823